ROTATION OF CROPS

About 1730, Lord Townsend introduced new methods in farming, including the rotation of crops and feeding root crops to cattle.

TOWN PLANNING
1700 - 1830

Whole parts of towns were re-planned and elegant houses, squares and terraces built.

ROAD IMPROVEMENTS

About 1750 new 'turnpikes' with a system of road maintenance and better road surfaces, provided for quicker coach travel and more efficient mail services.

THE RAILWAYS

From 1825 the railways developed quickly. Bridges, tunnels and cuttings were constructed to provide level tracks.

Series 663

OUR LAND IN THE MAKING — BOOKS 1 & 2

Some five hundred million years ago the land of Britain began to form from cooling molten rock. Through these millions of years it was shaped by gigantic natural processes; by volcanic eruptions, by upheavals in which land became ocean and ocean became land, and by the glaciers of the Ice Ages.

With the passing of the millions of years came plant life, then animal life and, about 250,000 years ago, man lived here. First came the hunters, then the food-gatherers or farmers and, gradually, the civilization we know.

That part of the story is told in Book I of OUR LAND IN THE MAKING. In this, the second book, the story is continued up to the present day, showing how almost all the changes are now being brought about by man.

A LADYBIRD BOOK OF

OUR LAND
IN THE MAKING

Book 2 : Norman Conquest to Present Day

by RICHARD BOWOOD
with illustrations by RONALD LAMPITT

Publishers: Wills & Hepworth Ltd., Loughborough
First published 1966   ©   *Printed in England*

The Lord of the Manor

When the Normans conquered England in 1066 they found a system of living already long established. It was based on the village community and we call it the manorial system. Every village was a self-contained community and belonged to the lord of the manor, who lived in the manor house with his land around it.

Some of the fields were the lord's own 'demesne', some were let to tenants, who paid for them partly in rent and partly in work, and some were divided into long narrow strips which were cultivated by the labourers, or villeins. Other land: such as woods, meadow and waste, was common land, shared by all the villagers for their cattle, pigs and poultry.

The villein virtually belonged to the lord of the manor, and was not permitted to go away. He paid no rent for his cottage and strip of land, but worked for the lord instead. He received no wages, but had the protection of the lord.

This way of life went on for three hundred years after the Norman conquest. We can still find traces of the strips of land the villeins cultivated, and names of fields and villages often remain in use to-day.

4   *A village community and Manor House.*

7214 0117 1

The Royal Forests

William I divided England between those of his friends who helped him conquer it in 1066, but also set aside great tracts of land for himself. He and his successors were all fond of hunting, and nearly a third of England was reserved as royal hunting forests. The New Forest in Hampshire is a royal forest which has remained. Windsor Great Park is another.

The land reserved for royal forests was usually too poor for farming, and had a great deal of rough heather-covered ground as well as trees. It was good for deer and boar-hunting but not for much else.

The deer still live in the New Forest, though they are not hunted any more, but the wild boars and the wolves which once lived there have long disappeared. The wild ponies were not there in Norman times.

The Norman kings made very strict laws to protect their forests. At one time a man could be hanged for killing a royal deer, or he could have his hand cut off. Nevertheless there were always some people who dared to poach the royal deer, as Robin Hood did in Nottingham Forest at a later date.

A royal forest.

Land of Sheep

A terrible disaster struck England in 1348, and had the effect of considerably changing the appearance of the countryside. The disaster was a plague called the Black Death, which was brought by rats in ships. Nearly half the people in England died of the infection, some villages were emptied by the death of everyone in them, and in others only a few survived.

It caused the break-up of the manorial system, because there were not enough people left to work the land in the old way. Land-owners had to do something else, so they changed to sheep farming, for a large flock of sheep can be looked after by one man. Gradually most of the cultivated land and the old villeins' strips became grass for sheep to graze, the fine, rich grass of England.

As the number of flocks increased a new prosperity came to England, the result of selling the wool abroad. The wool merchants became rich and the towns in good sheep country, like the Cotswolds, became rich too. You can see the proof of this in the old wool towns. They have wide streets with many fine houses, and splendid churches built by the rich wool merchants.

A Cotswold wool town.

Land Enclosure

When the land was cultivated under the manorial system, fields and strips were not all fenced. The only fencing was round the whole area to protect it from wild animals. When the land was used for sheep farming however, hedges, walls or fences were necessary to keep neighbours' flocks apart. If flocks became mixed up it was confusing and could have led to trouble. So land was enclosed, and with it much of the old common land.

The result was that many villagers lost their small plots of land, their strips and their shares in common land, so they had to work as labourers on the new farms or go to the towns to make a living. Many became spinners and weavers and made cloth from the abundant wool which had become available.

The 'land enclosure', as it is called, gave the countryside a different appearance between 1400 and 1600. It was nearer the appearance of to-day, with the pattern of fields separated by hedges, fences or stone walls.

The countryside after land enclosure.

The Market Town

Markets were authorized by Royal Charter to be held on certain days, Market Days, and the market was an important feature of the medieval town. On that day the country people took their produce to the town to sell in the market; butter, eggs, fruit and vegetables, wool, hides for leather, and many hand-made articles. Beasts and birds were also sold.

Many medieval towns were enclosed by high walls with gates, which were closed at night and guarded. There was always a church, a town hall and, often, a castle. Towns were usually built by rivers for the water supply.

Craftsmen plied their trades: butchers, leather-workers, cloth merchants, corn merchants, tailors, blacksmiths, goldsmiths and so on. Each had a sign hanging outside his house or shop. Although the houses were crowded close together many had gardens.

We can still find traces of the medieval town from which a modern one has grown; perhaps an ancient building, street names which have not changed and, most likely of all, the market place.

A medieval market place.

The Glory of our Cathedrals

The Normans were great builders, and some of their castles and cathedrals still stand. Their work can be recognized by the thick walls, the strong, sturdy pillars and the squat towers. The cathedrals are so strongly built that they look like castles.

England is famous for her beautiful cathedrals, and the finest were built after the Normans, in what is known as the Gothic period of architecture, between 1200 and 1500. Some of the Norman cathedrals were enlarged and many new ones were built.

The Gothic builders had a great advantage over the Normans, because they knew how to use the pointed arch instead of the round arch. This gave the cathedrals strength with lightness; they could build thin walls, use slender pillars and tall towers, sometimes topped by delicate spires. Very large windows were made in the walls. The Gothic cathedrals are miracles in stone, beautifully proportioned and exquisitely decorated. They have been in daily use for six or seven hundred years, and are among the glories of the land.

Gothic architecture.

GOTHIC ARCHITECTURE

PILLAR

WINDOW

CATHEDRAL

The Splendour of our Castles

Britain is rich in ancient castles; some are still family homes, some are royal castles, some are ruins which remind us of their past grandeur. The Normans built castles because they lived in a conquered land with enemies about them. But the greatest castles were built in the reigns of two strong and warlike kings, Edward I (1272-1307) and Edward III (1327-1377).

Edward I conquered Wales, which had successfully resisted the Normans, and brought it into his realm, and to keep this turbulent and independent people under subjection, he built great castles at strategic places.

The castles dominate the landscape over which they once held sway. Each castle has a keep, in which were the living quarters, and very strong walls and towers with a battlemented walk for sentries and soldiers in time of siege. The gate-house had a portcullis, which was lowered to prevent enemies getting in, and a drawbridge over the moat.

The barons of those days had their own armies and they too lived in strong castles, to defend themselves against enemies and jealous neighbouring barons.

An Edwardian castle.

Woods and Forests

Until about five hundred years ago a great part of England was forest and woodland, and many meadows and cornfields of to-day were once covered with trees. The few forests which remain were preserved because they were royal forests, but even they were reduced in size; Epping Forest was once more than ten times as large as it is now. Most others, like the Forest of Arden in Warwickshire, have quite disappeared.

There were three main reasons for the destruction of the forests. Before coal was available, the trees were cut down to make charcoal for smelting iron, and they were cut down for building houses, and, near the coast, for building ships.

Since Britain is an island she has always needed ships, and until a hundred years ago they were always built of wood. As England grew in importance she needed more ships for trading overseas and for her navy, and so more and more trees were felled. The great need for ships began in the reign of Queen Elizabeth I (1558-1603) when the New World—America— was being discovered and Englishmen sailed their ships all over the world.

The destruction of the forests.

DESTRUCTION OF FORESTS

for ship building

for smelting

for house-building

Schools and Colleges

The monasteries, of which there were once many all over England, were at one time the only places where children could be educated, and only if they were later to become priests or scholars within the organization of the church. As England grew prosperous and busy, however, men wanted their sons to learn to read, write and calculate, and clerks were needed for the offices of the merchants. Education became more general and after about 1450 many towns had a grammar school.

Kings, noblemen and rich merchants founded schools, and also colleges at Oxford and Cambridge. Many of the schools were at first intended to educate poor boys only, but as time passed they became very large and famous. King Henry VI founded Eton College in 1443 for 'twenty-five poor and indigent scholars', and he also founded King's College in Cambridge.

When the monasteries were demolished in 1536, more schools and colleges were founded and most of them are still in use, some as ancient grammar schools, others as large boarding schools.

King's College Chapel, Cambridge.

Stately Homes

All over Britain magnificent country houses stand in their fine parks. Some are still used by the families who own them, others have become schools or institutions, and many can be visited by the public.

Many of these 'stately homes' were built in the reign of Queen Elizabeth I, though some are even earlier. As conditions became more settled there was no need for people to live in strongly fortified castles, and the fine houses were built instead. They continued to be built for the next two hundred years. They were built as magnificently as possible to show the wealth and position of their owners.

The private parks were sometimes five miles round, enclosed by high walls or fences, with imposing gates and a lodge. Many of the parks were planned by Lancelot Brown (1716-1783), who was known as 'Capability Brown'. He designed the parks with carefully arranged trees and sometimes a building such as a grotto or a temple, to be pleasing to the eye and to add grace and dignity to the great house. These private parks are still a lovely feature of our countryside.

Parkland and stately homes.

PARKLAND DESIGNED BY 'CAPABILITY BROWN'

A STATELY HOME

'Turnip Townsend' and Farming

A great improvement was made in British farming between 1700 and 1800, when new scientific methods began to be introduced. The best known of the men who brought in new ideas was Lord Townsend, known as 'Turnip Townsend', who farmed in Norfolk between 1730 and 1738.

Lord Townsend introduced a way of using the land more profitably by growing in rotation turnips, barley, grass and wheat, thus avoiding the need to let land rest every third or fourth year. He also solved the problem of feeding cattle in winter. Previously, when grass stopped growing, farmers had to feed their cattle on hay and there was never enough, so most of the animals were killed, and the meat salted to prevent it going bad. Lord Townsend grew crops of turnips and stored them to feed the cattle in the winter, and so it was not necessary to slaughter so many.

The new methods of growing crops meant smaller fields, so hedges or walls divided up the old large fields, making the country look even more like it does now. The old borders were followed, however, and the field shapes of to-day often mark the edges of fields and cultivation strips of a thousand years ago.

More hedges and smaller fields change the appearance of the countryside.

Elegant Building

Britain's towns were given a new and an elegant appearance between 1700 and 1830. This period covers the building styles known as Queen Anne, Georgian and Regency, all three of them periods in which houses were very well designed.

Previously, towns had grown naturally and usually had a disorderly, higgledy-piggledy appearance. In the new age, architects planned whole parts of towns, and built beautiful houses in terraces, or in squares with gardens in the middle.

The houses of these periods are well-proportioned and dignified, with carefully spaced windows and handsome front doors. They can be seen in many towns, especially in London, Edinburgh, Bath, Cheltenham and Brighton.

Brighton became famous after 1784 when the Prince of Wales, later King George IV, went there regularly, and later built the Royal Pavilion. It became the fashion to go to the seaside. When railways made travel easy and fast, people adopted the habit of going to the seaside for their holidays, and seaside towns came into being, often growing from small fishing villages.

A Georgian seaside resort.

Roads Old and New

When the Romans went away from Britain in 410 A.D., their splendid roads were neglected and almost disappeared, and they were often replaced by narrow rutted tracks which rambled between villages and market towns, winding deviously along the borders of people's property.

The first important improvement was made about 1750 when 'Turnpike Trusts' were instituted. Each trust looked after a stretch of road and found the money for keeping it in good repair by making all road users pay a fee, or a 'toll'. The amount charged varied with the size of the vehicle, the number of horses, or the number of cattle or sheep. Toll gates were set up at each end of the stretch of road, and the toll gate keeper lived in a cottage with windows looking up and down the road. You can still see these old cottages.

Roads were further improved when a Scotsman named John Macadam (1756-1836) invented a method of making roads with a hard, smooth surface which would not become rutted. Many of the roads of old England still remain, following their leisurely course along tracks which have been used for more than a thousand years.

The toll gate and keeper's cottage of a ' turnpike '.

Coaches and Coaching Inns

The smooth road surface invented by Macadam improved communication in Britain at a time when good roads were particularly necessary to take the traffic of the rapidly increasing industry and trade. The macadamized roads of Britain were the fastest and best in the world.

Stage coaches, drawn by four matched horses, sped along the new roads at seven miles an hour, linking every town in the land. They ran to a strict time-table, summer and winter, with passengers inside and on top, and smart mail coaches with an armed guard carried the mail. The period between 1820 and 1836 was called the Golden Age of coaching.

Market towns and, where necessary, the villages in between, had coaching inns which performed the same service as railway stations. Horses were stabled at the inns and passengers could have a meal while the horses were changed for fresh ones for the next stage. Many of the old coaching inns still exist, and you can see the archway through which the coachman swung his horses after his passengers had eaten and rested.

A stage coach and coaching inn.

Power From Steam

In 1781 a young Scotsman named James Watt patented a new kind of steam engine. Steam engines had been in use for fifty years for pumping, but Watt's engine was something quite new and very important, for it turned a wheel so that machinery could be driven by the power of steam. Until then the only sources of power or energy were man-power, horse-power, windmills and water-wheels.

The steam engine brought about a revolution in man's way of life, and had world-wide effects. We call this the Industrial Revolution. With the new power, articles could be made in great quantities by machines in factories, instead of by hand by craftsmen in their homes.

Factories were built in cities and towns for countless industries—spinning cotton, weaving cloth, making machinery and for making every kind of commodity. The towns grew quickly, and houses had to be built for the workers. They were small houses packed closely together in mean streets. Britain became the richest and busiest country in the world, but the crowded smoky towns became an ugly feature in the beautiful landscape.

Early industrial towns mar the countryside.

'King Coal'

One reason for the great industrial prosperity of Britain was the plentiful supply of coal, for coal was an essential fuel for the engines which drove the machines. So vital was coal to the Industrial Age that it was called 'King Coal' and 'Black Gold'.

As we learned in Book I, when we read of the earliest phases in the development of Britain, three million years ago parts of the land were covered with forest. The dead vegetation from these was compressed through the millions of years to form the rock we call coal. The coal seams where it is found are now often hundreds of feet below the surface.

Industry naturally developed near the coal supplies. The steel industry of South Wales grew because both iron ore and the coal to smelt it could be found there. Many rich coalfields are in the Midlands and north of England, so it was there that industrial centres grew.

Where coal is mined the landscape is marked by large mounds of earth dug out of the mine, by heaps of waste and by pools caused by subsidence of the earth due to mining. Such districts often have a dirty and dreary appearance.

The dreary waste heaps and buildings of the early collieries.

The Canals

The first important canal was opened in 1761 to carry coal from the Duke of Bridgewater's coal mines at Worsley to Manchester, seven miles away. The Bridgewater Canal was followed by the construction of many others in the next fifty years until there was a whole network. They linked the manufacturing towns with coal-mines, ports and other towns, among them Manchester, Liverpool, Derby, Birmingham and London.

The canals were needed to carry coal and goods to the new and growing manufacturing towns; for the roads could not take the heavy traffic of horse-drawn wagons. Britain is well blessed with rivers, but they follow a winding course along valleys, while canals could be cut in direct lines from town to town.

One of the greatest canal-makers was Thomas Telford (1757-1834), and he and other brilliant engineers overcame all manner of difficulties. Canals go over hills by a system of locks, which raise the level step by step. They cross valleys on high aqueducts and go through mountains in tunnels. The canals were very busy with horse-drawn barges until the railways came and took their trade. There are still some three thousand miles of navigable rivers and canals in Britain, but they are little used to-day.

A canal and lock.

The Coming of the Railways

An event of the greatest importance to our land took place in 1825 when the first passenger railway line in the world was opened between Stockton and Darlington. Five years later the Liverpool and Manchester Railway was opened and only eight years after that more than one thousand, eight hundred miles of railway were in operation. The railways solved the problem of transporting coal and merchandise quickly.

Engineers and surveyors achieved miracles of construction as they built the railways to link every city and town. Foremost among them were George Stephenson (1781-1848), the pioneer designer of locomotives, and Isambard Brunel (1806-1859), the great builder of bridges.

The new railway lines cut boldly across the country. They had to be as level as possible, so embankments were built to cross low ground and deep cuttings were made through high ground; tunnels were bored through mountains, and bridges spanned valleys. All this brought new features to the landscape.

The railways revolutionized transport. Barges travelled at three miles per hour, horses at seven, but trains could travel at sixty miles an hour.

Railways make their mark on the landscape.

Water for the Million

Among the problems set by the rapid increase in the number of people in the land was the need for a plentiful supply of good water. Water is essential to life, and in older and simpler times men always made their homes near lakes, rivers, springs or wells. Villages and towns grew where the water supply was good.

But these natural sources became insufficient as the population grew. In 1800 the population of England and Wales was nine million, in 1900 it was thirty-two million and in 1950 it had risen to forty-three million, and it is still increasing. Water is supplied to this large population from reservoirs, or artificial lakes. A dam is built across one end of a valley so that it is filled by the rivers and streams which flow into it. The water is supplied through pipes to the town which the reservoir serves, where it is purified and flows through more pipes to the taps.

Big cities need so much water that sometimes very large valleys are flooded to make giant reservoirs, and villages and farms have to be drowned. The progress of the modern world usually spoils the beauty of the countryside, but reservoirs make lakes, often beautiful ones.

New reservoirs change the countryside.

The Ports of Britain

When the Romans came to Britain, nineteen hundred years ago, they found a number of ports to which ships had been sailing from the eastern Mediterranean for the purpose of trading. For the next four centuries these were used for the galleys and sailing ships which plied between Rome and her British colony. Many of our modern ports have grown from these ancient ones.

Ports are vital to Britain because she is an island, and they have always been used both for coastal trade between one part of Britain and another, and for trade with the rest of the world. The Industrial Revolution affected the ports as well as everything else. The factories needed more ships to bring raw materials and to carry finished products to foreign markets. The railways provided swift transport to and from the ports.

Modern ports are very large; the Port of London, for example, extends for sixty-nine miles. Ports have changed quiet estuaries and river-mouths into busy docks, with sheds, quays, cranes and a network of railway lines. They are the gateways to the outside world.

A modern port.

Airports

Just as ships need ports, and rivers and estuaries have become busy with docks, so aeroplanes need their ports, and large areas of country have been made into airports. An airport needs a large flat piece of land as near as possible to the city it serves. Railway stations were built in the middle of cities, but there is always a long journey from airport to city centre.

As the speed of aeroplanes increased, so did the length of the runways needed. Long concrete landing strips are made, which can be lighted at night. The airport buildings include the control tower, from which the pilots receive their landing instructions, passenger accommodation, and, as at sea ports, passport and customs offices. There must be sheds for mail and goods taken by air, and repair and maintenance sheds for the aircraft. Giant radar screens turn slowly round, scanning the skies. Airports are yet another addition imposed on the countryside by progress.

Larger planes make huge airports necessary.

Pylons Across the Land

It is only a little more than a hundred years since the scientist Michael Faraday (1791-1867) made the discoveries which gave mankind the new power of electricity. Like the invention of the steam engine and the locomotive, electricity has changed both our way of life and the look of the land.

In the power stations the dynamos which make the electricity are driven by coal or oil, by the energy of falling water (hydro-electric power) or, in the most modern power stations, by atomic energy. The electricity which is generated has to be delivered to the factories, towns and homes which use it. As water is taken from reservoir to tap through pipes, so electricity is taken along wires, or cables. Sometimes the cables are buried underground, but for long distances they are taken overground, carried on tall pylons. Electricity pylons have become another new feature of the countryside. The graceful steel pylons stretch in straight lines across the fields, taking electricity to towns, villages and farms. This is yet another way in which progress is changing the appearance of the land.

Electricity pylons stride across the countryside.

Roads and Motorways

The invention of the internal combustion engine at the beginning of the century, which also gave us the motor car, has made a great difference to our roads. They were improved two hundred years ago by the turnpike trusts, and later by the macadamized road surfaces which made the roads of Britain the best in the world at that time. As industry and population grew in the last century, the roads were not particularly affected because the railways took most of the new traffic.

When the motor car, the motor lorry and the motor bus came on the scene, however, the situation altered, and as the number of vehicles increased it was found that our roads were inadequate. Traffic became congested at road junctions and in towns.

Roads are being improved in every possible way and a new kind of road has come into being, the motorway, specially designed for heavy and fast traffic. A motorway is built straight across the land from town to town, as the Romans built their roads. There are no corners and no cross-roads; instead there are 'clover-leaf' junctions.

An old winding road and a modern motorway with clover-leaf junction.

New Towns

The very large increase in population in the past hundred years has completely changed the towns, and the population of the countryside has dwindled as people have gone to towns where wages are higher.

Old market towns which had changed slowly over many centuries have spread outwards as thousands of houses were built for the new population. Town planners often control new buildings to give towns a good and efficient design. Often land in a town is so scarce that buildings are made very high, to accommodate as many people as possible on the minimum ground space.

As more and more cars, lorries and buses come into use, traffic congestion in towns is a serious problem which can only be solved by new thinking in the planning of towns.

An example of the town of the future is Coventry, where the centre has been rebuilt. Traffic and pedestrians are kept apart. The shoppers use 'precincts' where there are no vehicles, and the roads are planned to let traffic flow smoothly.

A modern shopping precinct.

SOME MAIN INFLUENCES

MANORIAL SYSTEM
1066 - 1400

This was a system of self-contained villages each belonging to a Lord of the Manor.

EARLY LAND ENCLOSURE
1400 - 1600

Hedges, walls and fences were built to separate and protect sheep, etc.

SHIP BUILDING

From the reign of Queen Elizabeth I (1558 - 1603) timber was felled for the many merchant-ships required for overseas trade.

STATELY HOMES

Fortified dwellings were no longer necessary after about 1500, so wealthy people built fine houses in private parks.